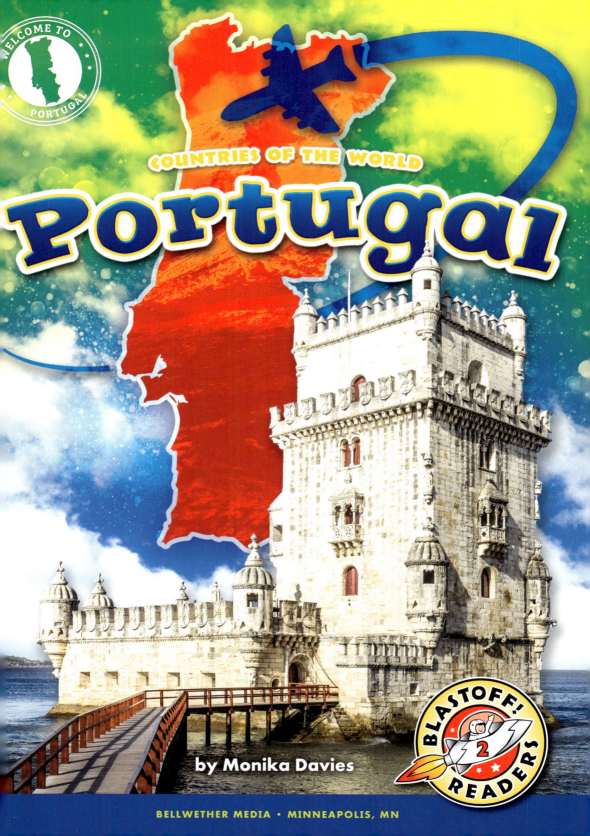

Blastoff! Readers are carefully developed by literacy experts to build reading stamina and move students toward fluency by combining standards-based content with developmentally appropriate text.

Level 1 provides the most support through repetition of high-frequency words, light text, predictable sentence patterns, and strong visual support.

Level 2 offers early readers a bit more challenge through varied sentences, increased text load, and text-supportive special features.

Level 3 advances early-fluent readers toward fluency through increased text load, less reliance on photos, advancing concepts, longer sentences, and more complex special features.

★ **Blastoff! Universe**

Reading Level

Grade K

Grades 1–3

Grade 4

This edition first published in 2025 by Bellwether Media, Inc.

No part of this publication may be reproduced in whole or in part without written permission of the publisher. For information regarding permission, write to Bellwether Media, Inc., Attention: Permissions Department, 6012 Blue Circle Drive, Minnetonka, MN 55343.

Library of Congress Cataloging-in-Publication Data

Names: Davies, Monika, author.
Title: Portugal / by Monika Davies.
Description: Minneapolis, MN : Bellwether Media, Inc., 2025. | Series: Blastoff! Readers : Countries of the world | Includes bibliographical references and index. | Audience: Ages 5-8 | Audience: Grades 2-3 | Summary: "Relevant images match informative text in this introduction to Portugal. Intended for students in kindergarten through third grade"– Provided by publisher.
Identifiers: LCCN 2024040113 (print) | LCCN 2024040114 (ebook) | ISBN 9798893042320 (library binding) | ISBN 9798893043297 (ebook)
Subjects: LCSH: Portugal–Juvenile literature.
Classification: LCC DP517 .D38 2025 (print) | LCC DP517 (ebook) | DDC 946.9–dc23/eng/20240923
LC record available at https://lccn.loc.gov/2024040113
LC ebook record available at https://lccn.loc.gov/2024040114

Text copyright © 2025 by Bellwether Media, Inc. BLASTOFF! READERS and associated logos are trademarks and/or registered trademarks of Bellwether Media, Inc.

Editor: Suzane Nguyen   Designer: Laura Sowers

Printed in the United States of America, North Mankato, MN.

Table of Contents

All About Portugal	4
Land and Animals	6
Life in Portugal	12
Portugal Facts	20
Glossary	22
To Learn More	23
Index	24

All About Portugal

Lisbon

Portugal is a small country that is part of a **peninsula**. It is in southwestern Europe.

Portugal's capital is Lisbon. It is nicknamed the City of Seven Hills!

Land and Animals

Many rivers cut across Portugal. Most flow into the Atlantic Ocean.

Hills cover the northwest. They rise into mountains in the northeast. Southern **plains** end in cliffs along the coast.

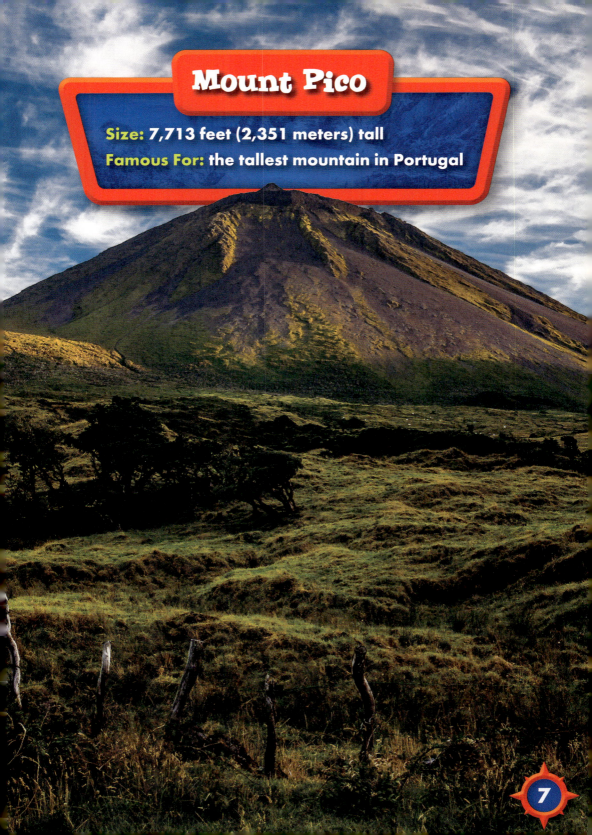

Mount Pico

Size: 7,713 feet (2,351 meters) tall

Famous For: the tallest mountain in Portugal

summer

In most of Portugal, winters are cool and wet. Summers are hot and dry.

8

It is cooler in the north. Snow only falls high in the mountains.

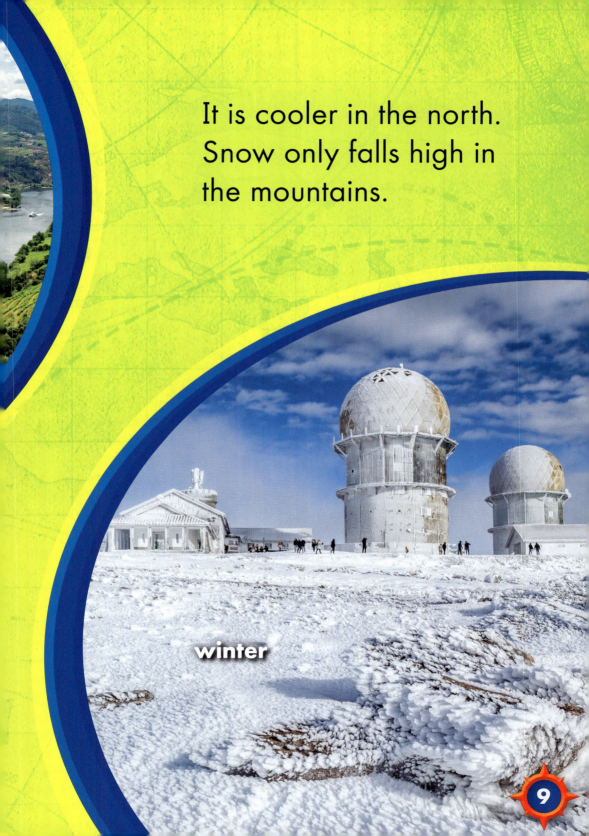

winter

Many animals call Portugal home. Wild pigs look for fruit. Lynx hunt in the forests.

Iberian lynx

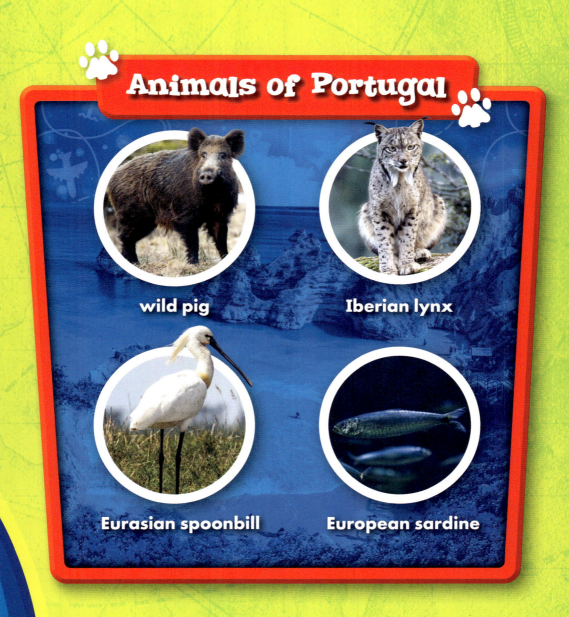

Animals of Portugal

wild pig

Iberian lynx

Eurasian spoonbill

European sardine

Spoonbills step in low waters. European sardines swim in the ocean.

Life in Portugal

Most people in Portugal are **ethnic** Portuguese. Nearly everyone speaks Portuguese. Many are **Roman Catholic**.

Most people live in cities. The largest is Lisbon!

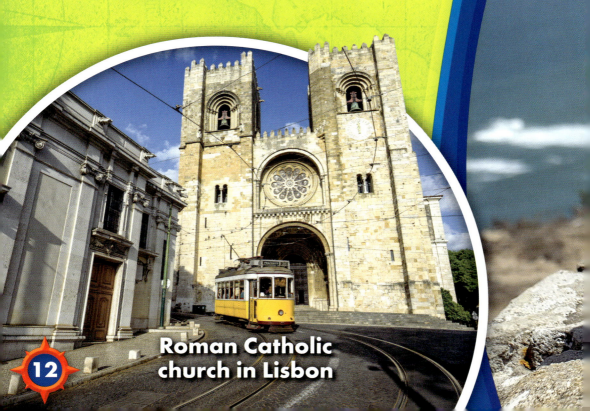

Roman Catholic church in Lisbon

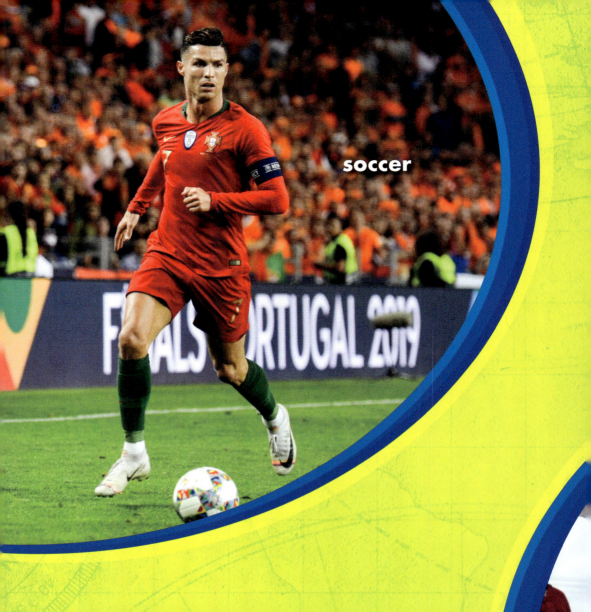

soccer

Soccer is popular in Portugal. Everyone cheers on their home team!

Music is important to Portuguese people. They sing and dance all over the country.

Seafood is part of most Portuguese meals. *Bacalhau* is salted cod fish. *Bacalhau com natas* is cod **casserole**.

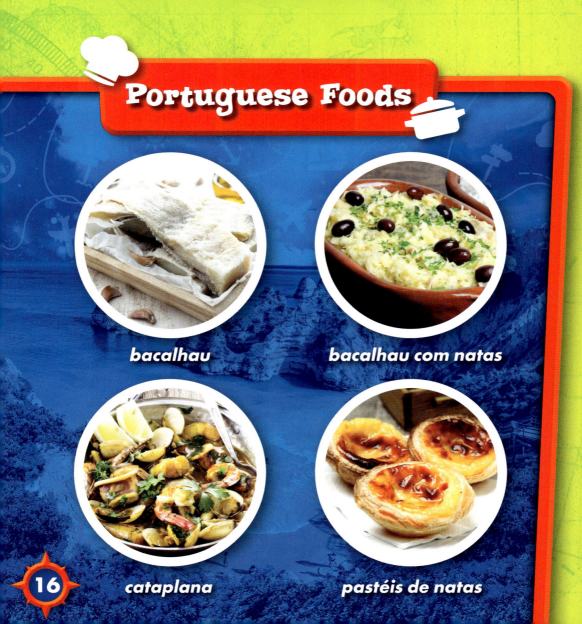

Portuguese Foods

bacalhau

bacalhau com natas

cataplana

pastéis de natas

seafood market

Cataplana is seafood and pork stew. *Pastéis de nata* is a yummy **custard** tart.

Liberty Day is on April 25. People carry carnation flowers. They watch parades.

Families **celebrate** Christmas together. They eat large meals and give gifts!

Liberty Day

Portugal Facts

Size:
35,556 square miles
(92,090 square kilometers)

Population:
10,207,177 (2024)

National Holiday:
Portugal Day (June 10)

Main Language:
Portuguese

Capital City:
Lisbon

Famous Face

Name: Cristiano Ronaldo

Famous For: soccer player

Religions

- other: 4%
- Protestant: 2%
- none: 14%
- Roman Catholic: 80%

Top Landmarks

Coimbra University

Jerónimos Monastery

Quinta da Regaleira

Glossary

casserole—different foods baked together and served in a wide dish

celebrate—to do something special or fun for an event, occasion, or holiday

custard—a sweet cooked mixture of milk and eggs

ethnic—related to races or large groups of people who share things such as customs, religion, and language

peninsula—a part of the land that sticks out from a larger piece of land and is almost completely surrounded by water

plains—large areas of flat land

Roman Catholic—people belonging to or relating to the Christian church that is led by the pope

To Learn More

AT THE LIBRARY

Adamson, Thomas K. *Soccer*. Minneapolis, Minn.: Bellwether Media, 2020.

Birdoff, Ariel Factor. *Portugal*. New York, N.Y.: Bearport Publishing, 2019.

Sabelko, Rebecca. *Mountains*. Minneapolis, Minn.: Bellwether Media, 2022.

ON THE WEB

FACTSURFER

Factsurfer.com gives you a safe, fun way to find more information.

1. Go to www.factsurfer.com.

2. Enter "Portugal" into the search box and click 🔍.

3. Select your book cover to see a list of related content.

Index

animals, 10, 11
Atlantic Ocean, 6, 11
capital (see Lisbon)
Christmas, 18, 19
coast, 6
Europe, 4
food, 16, 17
hills, 6
Liberty Day, 18
Lisbon, 4, 5, 12
map, 5
Mount Pico, 7
mountains, 6, 7, 9
music, 15
nickname, 5
peninsula, 4
people, 12, 14, 15, 18
plains, 6
Portugal facts, 20–21

Portuguese, 12
rivers, 6
Roman Catholic, 12
say hello, 13
snow, 9
soccer, 14
summers, 8
winters, 8, 9

The images in this book are reproduced through the courtesy of: milosk50, front cover; Millenius, p. 3; Sean Pavone, pp. 4-5; Balate.Dorin, p. 6; Robert van der Schoot, pp. 6-7; Mike Workman, pp. 8-9; Liliana Marmelo, p. 9; Jesus Cobaleda, pp. 10-11; WildMedia, p. 11 (wild pig); StockPhotoAstur, p. 11 (Iberian lynx); Alexxander, p. 11 (Eurasian spoonbil); Vladimir Wrangel, p. 11 (European sardine); Brois Stroujko, p. 12; tatyana_tomsickova, pp. 12-13; Vlad1988, p. 14; GeorgeVieriraSilva, pp. 14-15; Natalia Mylova, p. 16 (*bacalhau*); Brshutters, p. 16 (*bacalhau com natas*); hlphoto, p. 16 (*cataplana*); homeydesign, p. 16 (*pastéis de natas*); Greg Balfour Evans/ Alamy, p. 17; ZUMA Press Inc/ Alamy, p. 18; David_Evora, pp. 18-19; Tatohra, p. 20; Stefan Constantin 22, p. 20 (Cristiano Ronaldo); antonio gama, p. 21 (Coimbra University); saiko3p, p. 21 (Jerónimos Monastery, Quinta da Regaldeira); Svietlieishyi Andrii, p. 22.